LaNiyah Bailey presents

Stand Up!

"Bully Busters"...Coming to town

Educational Coloring & Activity Book

Created by: LaNiyah L. Bailey

LaToya "Toyiah Marquis" White & Laura Pérez Ricaud

ISBN-13: 978-0615540054
ISBN-10: 0615540058

Composition by Camp Pope Publishing

Author dedication

This book is dedicated to children all over the world who have ever been bullied or teased and decided to stand up for themselves. And to those who have ever been afraid to stand up, now's the time. You can do it, "Jessica" and "Diva-pup" say so!

About the author

Six year old author/youth advocate, LaNiyah Bailey was introduced to the world by way of NPR Radio after she and her parents appeared on Michel Martin's show "*Tell Me More.*" Broadcast in over 500 cities, it lead a world-wide discussion in support of President Barack Obama's anti-bullying initiative and the epidemic of Bullying in America, March 15, 2011. Shortly thereafter, her phone began ringing off the hook. Major media outlets such as CNN, FOX, NBC, BET, WGN, AOL, ABC, Huffington's Post and many others throughout the world, including London and Korea. They wanted to know more about this young girl's "inspiring courage" after she penned the highly-acclaimed children's book *Not Fat Because I Wanna Be* along with her mother LaToya "Toyiah Marquis" White and illustrator Laura Pérez Ricaud.

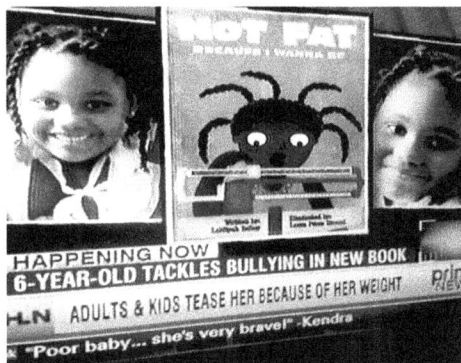

The book detailed the story of fictional character Jessica. Jessica was bullied because of her weight which was due to an underlying medical condition, which caused her to gain weight even though she was very, healthy and active. At such a young age Jessica had to endure some painful and un-happy times. Finally Jessica decided to stand up for herself.

The story was based on LaNiyah's very own true to life instances of being bullied and teased because of her weight. Since the book's release in March 2011, LaNiyah has been featured in magazines, in-terviewed on hundreds of radio shows, blogs and TV shows. The book has garnered "5-star reviews" across the board and is currently in lesson plans at schools throughout the United States and Korea.

You can find all of LaNiyah's books at: Amazon.com, BarnesandNoble.com, libraries, the author's official website: www.NotFatBecauseIWannaBe.com, and all major bookstores

6 year old author, LaNiyah Bailey is available for speaking engagements, interviews and events.

PR/Bookings Contact: Bookings@NotFatBecauseIwannaBe.com

LaNiyah thanks all of her supporters, family and friends. ☺

Love yourself! You are beautiful
no matter what anyone else says!

Bullying is **NOT** cool...

Peace...

Harmony...

Find 5 differences!

Color the scene using the color code

1: Yellow   **2: Brown**   **3: Violet**   **4: Black**   **5: Red**

Even though it may be hard,
you can stand up for yourself!

Help Jessica & Diva Pup find the 18 hidden words!

```
Y B E L I M S Z S D Y A J L Z
R R U L H P G D T U A N A J N
H P C L H P N O H B L G L V B
Q X L E L E E A O H P R R G A
M R C E I Y P Q W D V Y F N K
R I M R H P L I S D A B S I G
N E F K Y F T A V S M D W S K
L L H R C U D G U R G T Q A J
T Q Y C O N V O Y N H M V E N
W H U N A S C H O O L D U T P
K F V V X E E P Z N J G K Y E
B T F Y E H T A G H C E F G X
J K T J D Q T X H D K I N D Q
H S G N I L E E F G E Z V W R
M R O C Y L K T T W S F O E V
```

★ ANGRY   ★ BAD   ★ FRIENDS

★ CRY   ★ FEELINGS   ★ HAPPY

★ FUN   ★ KIND   ★ NICE

★ HELP   ★ SAD   ★ SCHOOL

★ PLAY   ★ TEACHER   ★ TEASING

★ SMILE   ★ BULLY

We are all different...

Find 5 differences!

Put the numbers in the correct box

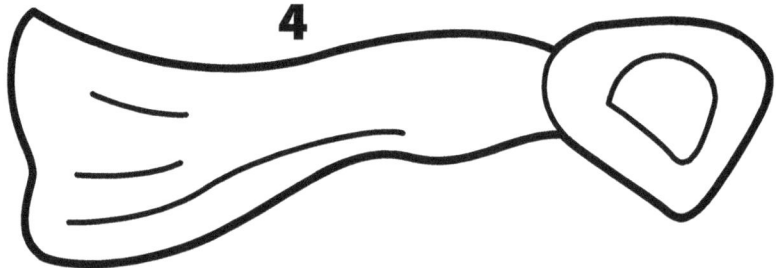

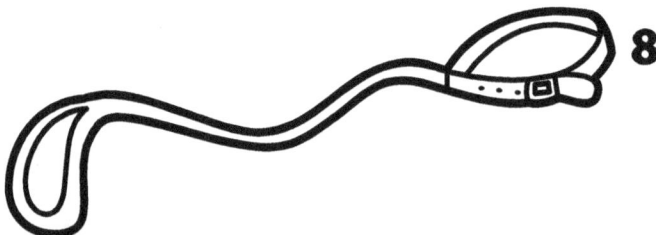

1

2

3

4

5

6

7

8

BB

DIVA

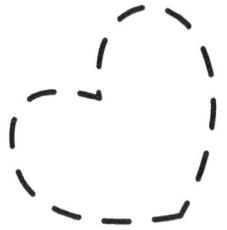

I'm sorry!

Jessica to the rescue!

It's not about how we look on the outside
It's the inside that counts

Oh my, I've lost my Diva-Pup!

Please help Jessica find her best friend Diva-Pup safely.

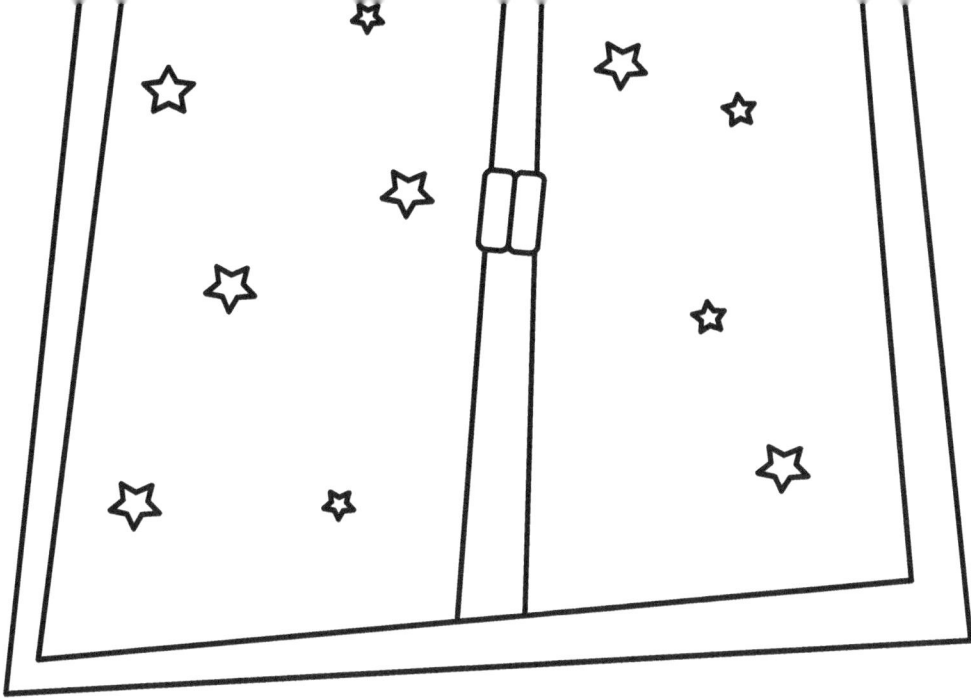

Bully Busters!

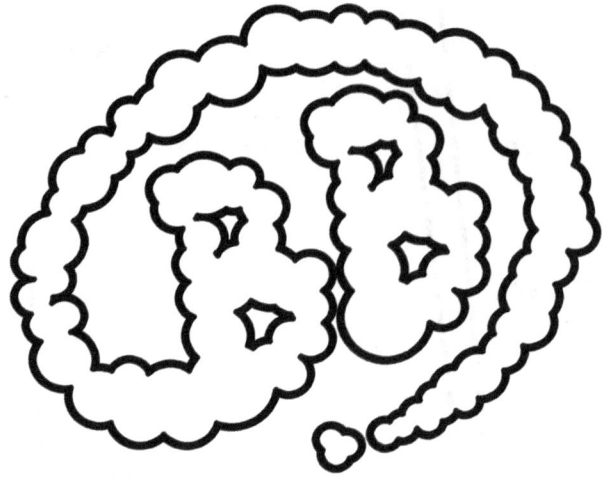

Sharing is caring!

Follow the numbers
and discover what's hidden

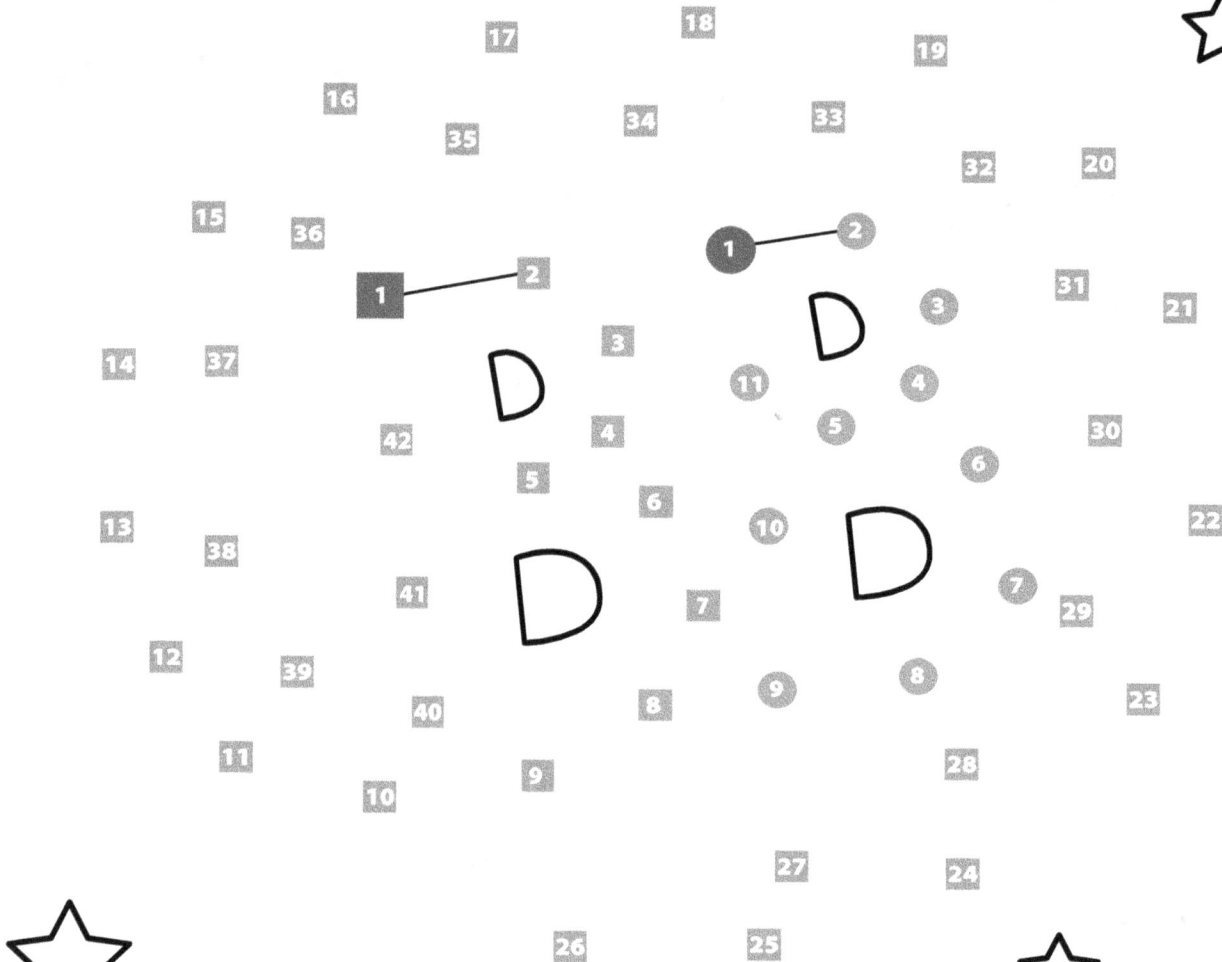

17 18 19

16

35 34 33

32 20

15 36 1 — 2 1 — 2 31 21

1 — 2 D 3

14 37 3 11 4 30

42 4 5 6

5 22

13 10

38 6

41 7 7 29

12 8

39 9 8 23

40 8

11 28

10 9 27 24

26 25

Word Scramble Game

Unscramble the words below to form words
that are associated with bullying

1. TINA YUIBLNIG _____

2. DSA _____

3. NUFIRNDYLE _____

4. NCEAPTCNACE _____

5. NEMA _____

6. ONT CEIN _____

7. EOLV UELSOYRF _____

8. SEEPRDINOS _____

9. GNISSASRAEBMR _____

10. LETL MOSENEO _____